MONKEY SEE, MONKEY DO

An Animal Exercise Book for You!

Anita Holsonback

with rhymes by Deb Adamson

Illustrations by Leo Timmers

The Millbrook Press
Brookfield, Connecticut

MONKEY

Jumping, swaying, fancy free,
a monkey hangs and swings in a tree.
Hands and feet can grab and cling,
the monkey walk is all bounce and swing.

ELEPHANT

Moving along, making its way
the elephant dines for hours each day.
Strolling and snuffing, munching on plants,
Wearing a suit with baggy gray pants.

FROG

Imagine your rump almost touching the ground,
your legs scrunched up tight, ready to bound.
When the time is right, you've got to think high—
you're looking to jump to a rock that's dry!

CROCODILE

Writhing slowly, slithering lowly,
the crocodile seems to struggle on land.
But this low-riding critter could not be fitter,
so, please, don't offer a hand.

FLAMINGO

Feathery light, pink and white,
legs that are strong, lanky and long.

DUCK

Waddle waddle everywhere, looky here, looky there.
Squish your body way down low, act as if you're in the know.
Now make sure the cars have passed,
and quack and flap across the grass.

CAT

Cats strut along without a care—
watching with a glance or stare.
Step lightly as the cat would do
and spring to safety from you-know-who!

GIRAFFE

Think of a giraffe's neck—graceful and strong.
Think of a giraffe's legs—really, really long.
Do you think things below look small
when you are extra, extra tall?

RABBIT

Dash, scatter, skip, flee,
hopping quickly under a tree.
Rabbits jump and rabbits zip,
and never, ever seem to trip.

RABBIT REVERSE

Bunnies would be surprised to see
a backward bunny hop from me.
Imagine a rabbit in reverse—
popping and bopping back feet first!

HORSE

Clippity clop, clippity clop,
this is the sound of a horse's trot.
Whinny snort, whinny neigh,
this is a horse who wants his hay!

SEAL

Slippery, slick and soaking wet,
whirling and swirling in the deep blue sea,
darting and diving on top of the waves—
A seal's life looks fun to me!

GORILLA

Hulky, bulky, chunky, strong.
Plenty of muscle and arms that are long.

KANGAROO

Kangaroo bounce
Kangaroo rocket
Kangaroo—don't forget the joey in your pocket!

BEAR

Powerful bears can stand upright
and claw with their paws at the trees.
Sometimes they find their favorite sweet
in a hive of honeybees.

CAMEL

Plodding and clomping through deserts of sand,
camels keep water close at hand.
It's stored in the humps upon their backs,
Like water bottles without screw-on caps.

TURTLE

Shell above, feet below,
a turtle can just wake up and go.
No need for clothes, no bed to make,
and just as much time as she wants to take.

CATERPILLAR

Be a caterpillar—hug a tree—
give each leaf a nibble.
And when you want to move along,
wiggle and wave your middle!

SWAN

Simple beauty to behold,
swans are graceful and grand.
Like a ballet on a stage
of water instead of land.

PENGUIN

Wings are short—can't take flight,
a silly sight in black and white.
Waddle, slip, slide and wiggle,
penguins really make you giggle.

GRASSHOPPER

Sometimes you see a grasshopper resting in the lawn.
Don't blink your eyes because if you do—POP!—he's gone.

SLOTH

Nighttime is the right time for the sloth to move around.
He's got no pressing business so he never makes much ground.
Dawdling and dallying he skulks among the trees,
hanging on with arms and legs and toes that come in threes.

DONKEY

Braying, honking donkey—holler to the world!
Drop your jaw—hee-haw.
Unleash your bucking backside high up in the air.
Why is it so much bothers you when others just don't care?

DEER

Stepping light, out of sight,
sometimes deer are filled with fright.
If they suddenly hear strange sounds,
away they go in leaps and bounds.

ANIMAL ACTIONS FOR BEGINNERS

MONKEY
With your hands and feet touching the floor, run like a monkey!

ELEPHANT
Keep your legs straight as you bend over and let your arms hang to the floor. Clasp your hands together to make your "trunk," and walk forward swinging your "trunk" along the floor from side to side.

FROG
Squat down with your hands on the floor in front of your feet. Swing your arms straight up by your ears and jump up as high as you can. Land on your feet again and gently bend your knees back into a crouch. Ribbit! Ribbit!

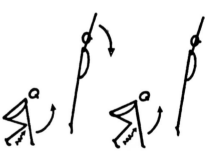

CROCODILE
Lie on your stomach with your legs straight and your arms bent, hands even with your head. Pull your right knee up toward your right shoulder. Push off with your arms and your right leg, and slide your body forward until your right leg is straight again. Now do the same with your left leg. Keep your hips on the floor when you move.

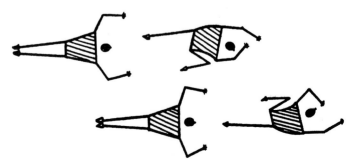

FLAMINGO

Lift your left foot and place it on the inside of your right knee. Try to jump forward on your right foot. Next try the other side. Give yourself a big hug now and you'll look like a real flamingo!

DUCK

Squat down on the balls of your feet with your back straight. Tuck your thumbs in your armpits. Walk forward with little steps while you flap your elbows. Quack!

CAT

Get on your hands and knees on the floor. Lift your feet off the floor and point them straight up. If you can walk forward on your knees with little steps, you can say "Meow!"

GIRAFFE

Hook your thumbs together and stretch your fingers to the side. Those are your ears, so put them way up above your head. Stand high on your toes, raise your chin, and walk forward on straight legs.

INTERMEDIATE ANIMAL ACTIONS

RABBIT

Stand with your arms straight back. Jump forward while you swing your arms straight toward the floor. Land on your hands about two feet away from where you started. Immediately push off your hands and land on your feet again. If you can't get the rhythm, try the bunny hop on the next page.

BUNNY

Sit in a squat with your hands on the floor in front of your feet. Move your hands ahead a little bit, then hop forward with your feet. Happy hopping!

RABBIT REVERSE

Stand with your arms straight back. Jump off your feet while you swing your arms straight forward to the floor. Land on your hands with your feet in the air and immediately push off with your hands and land on your feet. You might want to try the Backward Bunny first.

BACKWARD BUNNY

Sit in a squat with your hands on the floor in front of your feet. Hop back about 12 inches with your feet. Push off with your hands and place them in front of your feet again.

HORSE

Stand high on your toes and step forward with one foot, but stay on your toes and keep your legs straight. Lift your other knee high up to your chest, keeping your back straight. Repeat.

SEAL

Lie down on your stomach with your legs together. Lean on your elbows with your arms bent. Pull your body forward on your arms: left, right, left, right. Drag your legs behind you.

GORILLA

Stand with your legs straight. Bend your upper body forward and hold your ankles. Walk forward without bending your knees. Can you also keep your hips still?

KANGAROO

Stand with your upper body slightly forward and your legs slightly bent. Arms are straight back. Swing your arms forward while you jump, and land without straightening your upper body or legs.

BEAR

Bend over and put your hands on the floor. Can you keep your legs straight while you walk forward? Now try this with your hips straight as well.

CAMEL

Again, bend over and put your hands on the floor. While you walk forward this time, move the same hand and the same foot forward. Right hand moves with right foot, left with left. Keep your hips high.

ADVANCED ANIMAL ACTIONS

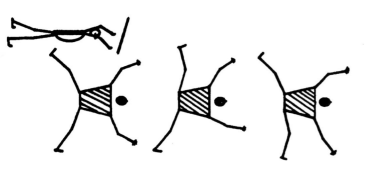

TURTLE

Lie down on your stomach and use your hands and knees to raise your body off the floor, heels pointed to the ceiling. Keep your arms and legs spread far apart and slightly bent. Move forward with your left hand and right foot, then with your right hand and left foot.

CATERPILLAR

Lie on your stomach and put your hands under your shoulders. Your legs should be straight, toes on the floor, heels up. Lift your hips and then push off your toes. Follow this movement by pushing off your hands and lifting your shoulders. Make a body wave, lowering your thighs, your hips, and then your shoulders. Can you crawl forward like a caterpillar?

SWAN

Stand with your arms straight out to the side. Step forward with your left foot. Slide your right leg sideways behind your left leg. Place your right hand on the floor and land on the outside of your right thigh. Slide your right arm parallel to your right leg. While you roll over your back from the right to the left shoulder, swing your left leg straight up and to the left, and then swing your right leg to the right. Step up with your right foot in front of your left leg. Practice this from left to right. You'll really feel like a swan once you can do this gracefully! If you can't quite get it, practice the Rhinoceros Roll, below.

RHINOCEROS ROLL

Stand with your fists against your forehead and your elbows against your stomach. Bend your legs and turn your knees to the left. Squat and drop onto the outside of your right thigh. Roll over onto your back from the right to the left shoulder. Place your right foot in front of your left leg and stand up. Can you roll over in a straight line? Can you also roll from left to right?

PENGUIN

Stand straight with your heels together and toes turned out. Keep your arms straight down beside your body and bend your wrists, lifting your hands parallel to the floor. Slightly lift up your left foot and your right heel, and turn your body to the right on the ball of your right foot. Then lift your right foot and left heel and turn your body to the left. You really have to squeeze the muscles in your bottom if you want to do this right!

GRASSHOPPER

Stand on your hands and toes with your heels lifted. Your weight should be evenly divided, your body horizontal to the floor and your legs slightly bent. Lower your whole body by bending your arms and legs even more, and jump, pushing with your hands and feet. Land on your hands and feet and repeat. Keep your body horizontal to the floor.

SLOTH

Stand on your hands and toes, legs slightly bent, fingers forward, weight evenly divided. Lift your left foot and your right hand up high at the same time. Moving very slowly (count to four), place each back down on the floor about 8 inches ahead of where you started. Now do the same with your right foot and your left hand. Move as slow as a sloth and don't fall over.

DONKEY

Stand with your arms straight. Place your hands about 8 inches in front of your feet on the floor. Push off with your feet and lift your hips up high, keeping your legs tucked in. Then kick your legs straight up while standing on your hands. Pull in your legs again and land on your feet. The closer you land to your hands, the easier it is to pop straight up. How often can you do the donkey kick without stopping?

DEER

From a standing position, push off your left foot, with your right knee pulled up tight to your chest. Swing your left arm forward and your right arm backward, both arms bent at the elbow. Straighten your left leg backward and swing it up. Then land on your right foot. Now jump off your right foot with your left knee pulled up tight. Your right arm swings forward, left arm swings backward. Keep leaping.

Library of Congress Cataloging-in-Publication Data
Holsonback, Anita.
[Van Apedraf Tot Kikkersprong. English]
Monkey see, monkey do: an animal exercise book for you! / by Anita
Holsonback, with rhymes by Deb Adamson; illustrations by Leo Timmers.
p.   cm.
Summary: Illustrated rhymes which describe aspects of animals are
followed by descriptions of moves, based upon animal locomotion, which a
young child can perform.
ISBN 0-7613-0260-3 (lib. bdg.)
1. Locomotion—Juvenile literature. [1. Animal locomotion. 2. Human
locomotion.] I. Adamson, Deb. II. Timmers, Leo, ill. III. Title.
QP301.H6713   1997
573.7'9—dc21   97-792   CIP   AC

First published in the United States in 1997 by
The Millbrook Press, Inc., 2 Old New Milford Road,
Brookfield, Connecticut 06804
First published in 1995 by Uitgeverij Clavis, Hasselt, Belgium
Copyright © 1995 Uitgeverij Clavis, Hasselt
All rights reserved

Printed in Belgium